HAUNTED HOTELS

AROUND THE WORLD

BY MEGAN COOLEY PETERSON

CAPSTONE PRESS

a capstone imprint

Snap Books are published by
Capstone, 1710 Roe Crest Drive,
North Mankato, Minnesota 56003.
www.mycapstone.com

For information regarding permission, write to Capstone, 1710 Roe Crest Drive, North Mankato, Minnesota 56003.

Library of Congress Cataloging-in-Publication Data
Names: Peterson, Megan Cooley, author.
Title: Haunted hotels around the world / by Megan Cooley Peterson.
Description: North Mankato, Minnesota : Capstone Press, [2017] | Series: Snap books. It's haunted! | Includes bibliographical references and index.
Identifiers: LCCN 2016034859| ISBN 9781515738589 (library binding) | ISBN 9781515738664 (ebook (pdf)
Subjects: LCSH: Haunted hotels--Juvenile literature. | Haunted places--Juvenile literature. | Ghosts--Juvenile literature.
Classification: LCC BF1474.5 .P48 2017 | DDC 133.1/22--dc23
LC record available at https://lccn.loc.gov/2016034859

Editorial Credits

Mari Bolte, editor; Kristi Carlson, designer; Wanda Winch, media researcher; Gene Bentdahl, production specialist

Photo Credits

Alamy: David Angel, 22, Franck Fotos, 10, Joe Devenney, 19, picturelibrary, 16, Q-images, 24; AP Images: Steven Senne, 13; Courtesy Long Island Paranormal Investigators, 6 (bottom); Dreamstime: Therealdarla, 9; Getty Images: Hulton Archive/ London Stereoscopic Company, 14, The Boston Globe/David Kamerman, 18, The LIFE Images Collection/Richard Howard, 12; Henry Yau, 8; North Wind Picture Archives, 21; Photos courtesy of 1886 Crescent Hotel & Spa, Eureka Springs, Arkansas, 26 (all), 28, 29; Shutterstock: Andreas Gradin, cover (top), A-R-T, calligraphic design, Blue Vista Design, lightning, Brooke Becker, round frame, Daniel M. Nagy, 17 (middle), Fantom666, grunge background, Gwoeii, 5, HiSunnySky, floral background, Hitdelight, 25, ilolab, brick wall, jakkapan, retro frame design, janniwet, ornate frame, kzww, wood background, Lario Tus, 23, Leremy, ornate sign design, LilGraphie, photo corners design, LovArt, globe design, maoyunping, 20, Nelson Sirin, 6, PeterPhoto123, oval frame, pictureguy, cover (middle), rayjunk, antique frame, Shanti Hesse, cover (middle), spaxiax, stone wall background

Printed in China.
092016   007892

TABLE OF CONTENTS

NO VACANCY

You're on a road trip with your family. Suddenly the car's engine sputters and dies. As your family walks along the highway, you spot a crumbling brick hotel. Inside, the innkeeper quickly gives you a key and sends you to your room.

As you're drifting off to sleep, you hear a loud bang. The lights flicker on and off again. The temperature in the room drops, and you can see your breath. A strange shadow moves past the foot of your bed. Could it be real? Or do you just need a good night's sleep?

Haunted hotels and inns have been reported for hundreds of years. Some people believe the **spirits** of the dead can return to Earth. They say ghosts often haunt the places where they died. The hotels in this book are said to be some of the spookiest places on Earth. Witnesses say the ghosts checked in and never left. Are these places really haunted? Or do people just enjoy a good ghost story? You decide.

With their long histories and thousands of guests checking
in and out, hotels are often sites of ghostly activity.

spirit: the invisible part of a person that
contains thoughts and feelings

THE STANLEY HOTEL
ESTES PARK, COLORADO, USA

The Stanley Hotel opened in 1909. It is still
operating today.

Inventor F.O. Stanley suffered from tuberculosis, an illness that affects the lungs. His doctor advised him to move somewhere out west, with clean, dry air. Stanley chose Colorado. The remote mountain setting inspired Stanley to build the Stanley Hotel. The hotel boasted electric lights, running water, and a skilled staff. No expenses were spared. But tragedy would soon strike.

Only two years after the hotel opened, a thunderstorm tore through the area. The hotel lost power. The guests were ushered to the lobby while employees lit the gas lamps. The staff was unaware that the odorless gas had begun to leak.

Chambermaid Elizabeth Wilson carried a lit candle as she walked the halls. When she opened the door to room 217, there was huge explosion. The blast allegedly sent Elizabeth crashing into the dining room below. Some news reports said she escaped with two broken ankles. Others said she was killed instantly.

Elizabeth's ghost may still haunt room 217. Guests have claimed her ghost folds their clothes and puts them away. Others reported Elizabeth's ghost climbing into bed with them.

SECRETS UNCOVERED

For years the story of room 217 was a mysterious tale that was retold with details substituted or changed from person to person.

In 2014 a worker made a discovery that gave the story some real-life credibility. Chunks of wallpapered drywall and carpeting were found in the hotel's basement. The wallpaper had a floral pattern in bold colors. The carpet was green with specks of red and blue. Historians found photos of room 217 taken before the explosion. The wallpaper and carpet they discovered matched the room's original décor, proving that the explosion had, in fact, happened.

HOME SWEET HOME

F.O. Stanley and his wife Flora loved their hotel. Some say they became permanent residents after their deaths. Photos taken in the billiard room reportedly captured Stanley's ghost. Flora's old piano sits in the hotel's music room. It is said to play by itself in the dead of night. Is Flora making music from the afterlife?

In April 2016 a hotel guest captured a ghostly figure at the top of the stairs with his cell phone camera.

FACT

Halloween is room 217's most popular night. Guests book the room years in advance

THE FOURTH FLOOR

Today people from around the world visit this allegedly haunted hotel. The fourth floor has its share of spooky stories. Guests report children laughing and running in the hallways. But when they check the halls, nobody is there. A young boy's ghost is said to pull blankets from the bed in room 408.

HOTEL OF HORRORS

Horror writer Stephen King stayed at the Stanley Hotel in 1974. King had heard rumors that it was haunted. He wanted to experience the Stanley for himself.

King arrived the night before the hotel closed for winter. He was the only guest. King stayed in room 217. He roamed the empty halls. King's night at the Stanley inspired his bestselling novel *The Shining*. Published in 1977, it was later made into a movie.

LIZZIE BORDEN BED & BREAKFAST
FALL RIVER, MASSACHUSETTS, USA

Guests to the Lizzie Borden Bed & Breakfast can take a one-hour tour of the home.

In August 1892, a grisly double murder shocked Fall River, Massachusetts. Businessman Andrew and Abby Borden had been hacked to death in their home. The main suspect? Andrew's adult daughter, Lizzie.

The day of the murders started like any other. The family had breakfast. Andrew left the house on business. Lizzie and her stepmother, Abby, stayed home.

The Borden's maid, Bridget Sullivan, spent the morning cleaning the windows. When Andrew returned home a few hours later, Bridget let him in at the front door. According to Bridget, no one else came to the house.

Around 11:15 a.m., Bridget heard Lizzie shout, "Father's dead!" Andrew had been killed with a hatchet in the parlor. A neighbor soon found Abby dead in an upstairs bedroom. Stories spread that Lizzie never got along with her stepmother. And although Andrew was wealthy, he apparently didn't share his money with Lizzie.

Lizzie was arrested for murder. Her trial lasted 15 days. The public was fascinated, and the newspapers only built on the drama around the case. But in the end, there wasn't enough evidence, and the jury found her not guilty. Lizzie spent the rest of her life as an outcast.

THE CASE AGAINST LIZZIE

The police had little evidence against Lizzie. She burned a dress shortly after the murders, claiming it was old and covered with paint—or was it blood? Nobody could prove either way. Although police recovered part of a hatchet in the basement, the murder weapon was never found. All of the doors were locked from the inside on the day of the murders. Only the kitchen's screen door was open, and Lizzie admitted to opening it.

The Borden house is equipped with ghost cameras.
Ghost hunters from around the world can tune in for
the chance to see the supernatural.

SPEND THE NIGHT ... IF YOU DARE!

The Borden house was opened as a bed and breakfast
in 1996. Guests can spend the night in Lizzie's old bedroom.
Brave guests sleep in the bedroom where Abby was murdered.
Even groups are welcome—the entire second and third
floors can be rented. Many guests at the house hope to see
something **paranormal**. Some host **séances**. Others wait for the
ghosts to come to them naturally.

paranormal: having to do with an unexplained event
séance: a meeting to contact the spirits of the dead

A visit to the Borden house isn't for those easily frightened. Doors open and close on their own. Lights flick on and off. Objects fall from tables and dressers in the night. A figure wearing Victorian clothing has been spotted in mirrors. In Lizzie's old bedroom, cameras suddenly stop working. Some visitors have felt something, or someone, sit on their beds. It is not uncommon for guests to flee in the middle of the night.

FACT

There is a famous poem about Lizzie Borden:
Lizzie Borden took an axe
And gave her mother forty whacks.
When she saw what she had done
She gave her father forty-one.

Crime scene photos from Lizzie's trial are displayed around the house.

LANGHAM HOTEL
LONDON, ENGLAND

The Langham was Europe's first "Grand Hotel".

Opened in 1865, the Langham Hotel was London's most opulent hotel. Guests arrived from around the world. But the hotel would soon gain a frightening reputation.

According to **legend**, a doctor and his wife died in room 333. Another story tells the tale of a German prince jumping out of a fourth-floor window. Maybe these spirits never left the hotel.

In 1973 James Alexander Gordon claimed a bright ball of light appeared in room 333. The light slowly changed into a man with silver hair and black holes for eyes. Other guests have reported similar experiences there—room 333 is now said to be the most haunted room in the city. One guest fled after a ghost rapidly shook the bed. Others have claimed to see a ghost wearing a military jacket.

In 2014 members of England's cricket team checked into the hotel. One player claimed his room was so hot, he couldn't sleep. Suddenly the bathroom faucet turned on—by itself. When the player turned on the light, the faucet turned off. He switched off the light, and the faucet turned on again. Many members of the team asked to switch rooms.

FACT

The ghost of **emperor** Napoleon III—a frequent hotel guest during his exile from France—is said to haunt the hotel's basement. Witnesses say his ghost makes eerie noises and steals equipment.

legend: a story handed down from earlier times that could seem believable

emperor: a male ruler of a country or group of countries

RUSSELL HOTEL
SYDNEY, AUSTRALIA

A hospital once stood where the Russell Hotel is today.

If you're looking for a good night's sleep, don't stay in room 8 at the Russell Hotel. Built in 1887, the hotel was frequented by sailors. One man seems to have claimed the room as his own. Guests reported waking up to find a ghostly deckhand standing at the foot of the bed, watching guests while they sleep.

FACT

Hotel guests can take a Tour of The Rocks to hear stories of murder, suicide, hauntings, and ghosts.

Employees at the hotel have also experienced ghostly activity. They report feeling sudden drops in temperature throughout the hotel. A phantom maid, wearing old-fashioned clothing, is said to walk the halls. Another ghost walks the halls too—creaking footsteps are heard up and down the hallways. But when people go to check on the noise, nobody is there.

A NIGHT AT THE RUSSELL

In 2015 journalist Lucy Thackray spent the night in room 8. She wanted to see if anything strange would happen. Thackray awoke around 4 in the morning. She claimed an intense pressure kept her in her bed. It felt as though someone—or something—was holding her down.

HAWTHORNE HOTEL
SALEM, MASSACHUSETTS, USA

In 1990 a séance was held in the hotel ballroom. Guests
hoped to summon the ghost of Harry Houdini.

The Hawthorne Hotel offers its guests more than just room
and board. The hotel is also said to be teeming with ghosts.

Long before the hotel opened in 1925, the Salem Marine
Society building stood in its place. When it was torn down,
the society's headquarters moved into the hotel. Ghosts of
sailors and captains have been reported floating around the
hotel ever since. **Vintage** maps and charts are kept locked up
inside the society's storage spaces. Witnesses claim they are
often found in disarray. Are the dead sailors itching to set
sail again?

A WITCH'S APPLE

Bridget Bishop was the first person accused of being a witch during the Salem Witch Trials. She was sentenced to die and was hanged in 1692. Legend has it that the hotel was built on an apple orchard once owned by Bishop. Many guests report smelling apples throughout the hotel.

Bridget Bishop is remembered at the Salem Witch Trials Memorial.

FACT

The TV show *Ghost Hunters* visited the Hawthorne in 2007. They did not experience any ghostly activity.

vintage: from the past

Room 325 is one of the hotel's most haunted areas. Guests claim lights turn on by themselves. Unseen hands turn on the bathroom faucet. Some guests say ghostly hands grabbed them while they slept.

Visitors and staff report cold spots around the hotel. One guest said a closet door opened by itself. Then a shopping bag on the bed crumpled, as if squeezed by invisible hands.

Even the employees can't escape the ghostly activity. After setting up tables in the basement, a worker left the room. When he returned, the chairs were stacked in a pyramid. The worker left and never went back to the hotel.

Chandeliers move and shake on the hotel's 6th floor.

Salem is best-known for the witch trials of 1692 and 1693. Hundreds of people were accused of being witches as their friends and neighbors turned them in. Many were thrown in jail, where they sometimes waited there for months while they waited for their trials. Some people died waiting. Prisoners included pregnant women, small children, and the elderly.

In total, 19 men and women were hanged outside the town at a place called Gallows Hill. The exact location of Gallows Hill is unknown today.

When the governor's wife was accused, the trials were stopped. Eventually the "witches" were pardoned and their rights restored. But the crimes had been committed. Some of the victims cursed their accusers before their executions. Could those curses have been real?

Accused witches could confess to witchcraft and be released, or refuse and face imprisonment.

SKIRRID MOUNTAIN INN
WALES, UNITED KINGDOM

The Skirrid Mountain Inn is one of the
oldest pubs in Wales.

Dating back to the 1100s, the Skirrid Mountain Inn in Wales doubled as a courthouse. Convicted criminals were hanged from a beam inside the building. Although their bodies were removed, their spirits may have stayed behind.

FACT

The last criminal was hanged at the inn around 1658. About 182 people were executed there.

Simon Curwood had a frightening experience at the inn. While eating lunch, he felt a pain in his stomach. He saw visions of people dying. In some of the visions, he was the person dying. He said he could feel their final moments. His is only one of the many similar tales about Skirrid Mountain Inn. Other guests have reported feeling ropes tightening around their necks. The ghostly ropes have even left marks on their skin.

The inn's most famous ghost is a woman named Fanny Price. She allegedly worked at the inn in the 1700s. She often makes herself known to female guests. One guest said Fanny's ghost tried to drown her in the bathtub. The guest fled the inn, still wet from the bathwater.

With a history dating back more than 900 years, it's no wonder ghosts choose the inn as their final haunting place.

HOTEL PROVINCIAL
NEW ORLEANS, LOUISIANA, USA

The Hotel Provincial stands at the heart of New Orleans.

Before this haunted hotel served travelers, soldiers used the buildings as a hospital. Wounded and dying men were brought there during the War of 1812 and the Civil War (1861–1865)—plenty of opportunities for ghosts to be left behind. Ghostly doctors with bloody aprons roam the grounds, perhaps looking for the ghosts of bandaged soldiers that also make themselves known.

The Hotel Provincial was opened in 1961. There are five buildings on the grounds. Much of the ghostly activity is said to happen in building 500. Guests claim to see bandaged soldiers moaning in pain in their rooms, or bloodstains that appear, then disappear, on furniture. Invisible hands pulled one guest from her bed. Doors open and close by themselves.

A security guard had quite a fright in building 500. He rode the elevator to the second floor. When the doors dinged open, he found he was not alone. The floor was filled with nurses tending to wounded Confederate soldiers.

Rumor has it that one hotel ghost loves music. The radio often turns—on its own—to his favorite country station.

FACT

The original 500 building served as a military hospital in the early 1700s. It was owned and operated by a group of nuns.

CRESCENT HOTEL
EUREKA SPRINGS, ARKANSAS, USA

The Crescent Hotel is nestled in the Ozark Mountains. It opened in 1886.

The Crescent Hotel might be the most haunted hotel in the United States. Guests in the late 1800s enjoyed riding through the mountains on one of the hundred horses provided by the hotel. A live orchestra entertained them during lavish meals. Afternoon teas and evening dances kept them busy in between.

Life at the hotel took a grisly turn in 1937. Norman Baker turned the Crescent into a hospital. Baker had no medical training. Still, he told the world he had discovered a cure for **cancer**. Baker's treatment did not cure cancer. Many of his patients grew sicker. Some died. But Baker became rich peddling his fake cure.

After Baker's arrest in 1940, the hotel seemed to sit empty. But when the Crescent reopened in 1946 many staff members and guests claimed to see ghosts from an earlier time period. In 1885 a worker named Michael allegedly fell to his death during the hotel's construction. He died in what is now room 218. Michael's spirit is said to pound on the walls and turn off lights. Some guests said ghostly hands reached out of a mirror. One guest reported hearing someone whispering "Michael" in her ear.

When the hotel opened in 1886, a man named Dr. Ellis joined the staff. He cared for sick guests. Room 212 was his office. A ghostly man dressed in Victorian clothing has been seen walking into the room—right through the closed door.

FACT

Norman Baker ran a cancer hospital in Iowa before leasing the Crescent Hotel. He "treated" patients for more than a decade.

cancer: a disease in which cells in the body grow faster than normal and destroy healthy organs and tissues

A ghost named Theodora haunts room 419. Staff says the ghost introduces herself as a cancer patient. Then she disappears. Some guests claimed their clothes had been packed overnight. Did Theodora's ghost lend a helping hand from beyond the grave?

Norman Baker's old **morgue** still resides in the hotel's basement. Baker performed **autopsies** on dead patients. The TV show *Ghost Hunters* explored the morgue in 2007. They captured the outline of a man on film. Was it the ghost of a former patient?

The hotel held a grand re-opening for the morgue in 2013.

Visitors during the hotel's ESP weekend can participate in guided tours and ghost hunts in the hotel's most active spaces.

IS IT REALLY HAUNTED?

No one knows for sure if haunted hotels exist. Studies show people are more likely to see ghosts *after* they've been told a place is haunted. Creaking floorboards or leaky faucets might be blamed on ghosts. Are you brave enough to stay at an allegedly haunted hotel? You might want to sleep with the lights on, just in case.

> **morgue:** a place where dead bodies are kept temporarily
>
> **autopsy:** an examination performed on a dead body to find the cause of death
>
> **ESP:** extrasensory perception; the ability to communicate with the paranormal

GLOSSARY

autopsy (AW-top-see)—an examination performed on a dead body to find the cause of death

cancer (KAN-suhr)—a disease in which cells in the body grow faster than normal and destroy healthy organs and tissues

emperor (EM-puhr-uhr)—a male ruler of a country or group of countries

ESP—extrasensory perception; the ability to communicate with the paranormal. Also known as the sixth sense.

legend (LEJ-uhnd)—a story handed down from earlier times that could seem believable

morgue (MORG)—a place where dead bodies are kept temporarily

paranormal (pair-uh-NOR-muhl)—having to do with an unexpected event that has no scientific explanation

séance (SAY-ahns)—a meeting to contact the spirits of the dead

spirit (SPIHR-it)—the invisible part of a person that contains thoughts and feelings; some people believe the spirit leaves the body after death

vintage (VIN-tij)—from the past

READ MORE

Doeden, Matt. *The Queen Mary: A Chilling Interactive Adventure*. North Mankato, Minn.: Capstone Press, 2017.

McCollum, Sean. *Handbook to Ghosts, Poltergeists, and Haunted Houses*. North Mankato, Minn.: Capstone Press, 2017.

Owings, Lisa. *Ghosts in Hotels*. Ghost Stories. Minneapolis: Bellwether Media, Inc., 2017.

INTERNET SITES

FactHound offers a safe, fun way to find Internet sites related to this book. All of the sites on FactHound have been researched by our staff.

Here's all you do:
Visit *www.facthound.com*
Type in this code: 9781515738589

 **Super-cool stuff!** Check out projects, games and lots more at **www.capstonekids.com**

INDEX

READ ALL THE IT'S HAUNTED TITLES!
Titles in This Set